DON'T LET YOUR FEARS STAND IN THE WAY OF YOUR DREAMS

NO FEAR

DESIGN BY JACQUELINE JONES DESIGN

WARNER BOOKS

A Time Warner Company

No Fear

Warner Books, Inc., 1271 Avenue of the Americas, New York, NY 10020

W A Time Warner Company

Printed in the United States of America
First Printing: November 1995
10 9 8 7 6 5 4 3 2 1

Library of Congress Cataloging-in-Publication Data
No fear : Don't let your fears stand in the way of your dreams.
      p. cm.
   ISBN 0-446-52026-8
    1. Sports — Psychological aspects — Quotations, maxims, etc.
2. Motivation (Psychology) — Quotations, maxims, etc. I. No Fear (Firm)
GV706.4.D65 1995   95-31463
796´.01 — dc20   CIP

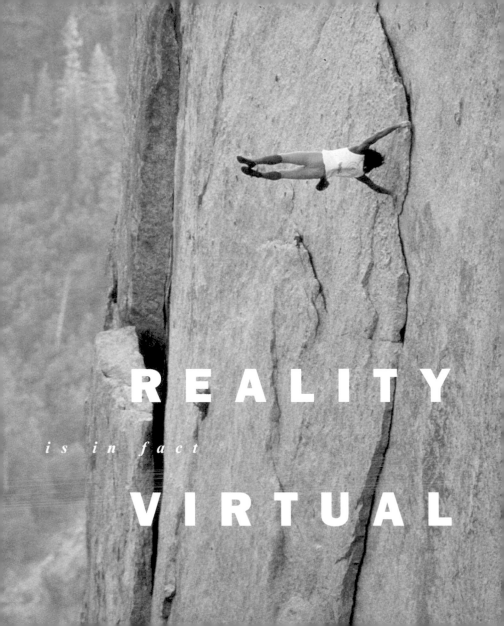

REALITY

is in fact

VIRTUAL

THE EXACT POINT OF CONTACT, PHYSICAL AND PSYCHOLOGICAL, BETWEEN MAN AND HIS SPORT. THAT IS WHERE THE GAME IS. IN THE BLEEDING, BROKEN HANDS REFUSING TO LET GO BECAUSE THERE'S STILL TIME ON THE CLOCK, TIME FOR ONE MORE PLAY. THAT IS THE TEST. THIS MEASURE OF COMMITMENT AND WHERE-WITHAL OF MIND AND BODY. IT IS NOT ON THE SCOREBOARD OR ON VICTORY LANE. THOSE ILLUSTRATIONS EXIST ONLY TO MAKE THE GAME EASIER TO UNDERSTAND FROM THE BLEACHERS, FROM LIVING ROOMS, FROM THE OUTSIDE LOOKING IN.

ONLY WHEN WE GET CLOSE DO WE LEARN WHERE THE GAME IS TRULY PLAYED. IT IS THIS INTIMACY THAT TAKES US PAST THE *MANO A MANO*, THROUGH THE OBVIOUS BATTLES WITH GRAVITY, SPEED AND THE ELEMENTS, TO EXPOSE THE VULNERABILITIES ALONGSIDE THE VICTORIES. AND IT IS HERE THAT WE DISCOVER ONE SIMPLE TRUTH ABOUT COMPETITION: IN SPORT AS IN LIFE, THE REAL OPPONENT, THE ONLY REAL ENEMY, IS WITHIN.

It's what we don't see. The Kevlar body armor, the metal braces, the hundred feet of bandage wrapping the cowboy's every joint under the leather and denim. **It's the subtlety of the events** behind the chute. How a particularly rank bull will change among the men preparing the rider. How the cowboy will subconsciously check off his tiny rituals of hat adjustments, and where and when to aim his tobacco-stained spit. **It's what we don't hear** in the dialogue of guttural grunts between the animal and the man as they establish the tone of their brief relationship. **It's the fact that we can't see the irony** in the lengths to which the man will go to fasten himself to the bull. The rope. The glue. **It's the look in the cowboy's eyes** as he nods his approval for the gate to swing open. That's when we first sense the line he crosses between the relative safety of the chute and the uncertainty of the arena. We still can't see it. But that line exists.

It is the point of
no return.

Commitment isn't the time you spend.

It's a line you **cross.**

It's the **difference** between

sitting on an **angry** bull

and having **your hand**

roped to his back.

WHERE I COME FROM,

there is no next time,

there is no second chance,

there is no time-out.

Whatever the fear may be

ook it in the eyes.

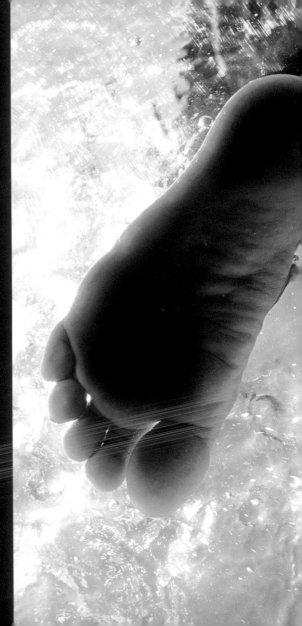

It is when we recognize the simplicity of surfing that we begin to see it past the clichés of beaches, bikinis and blond hair. It is the sight and sound of a three-story building being tossed from the sea, collapsing on a remote shore and engulfing a man armed with nothing but a board.

Now we begin to understand it. We begin to realize

that surfing wasn't born in travel brochures or on Hollywood sets. It was born when a man somewhere decided to tempt the ocean. He was as naked then as now, paddling out into one of nature's greatest unknowns. And when he jumped to his feet and first rode down that mountain of water, he was perhaps as close as man will get to walking on it.

The past, the
and the
between

present
journey

IT'S THE BLADES. THEY ACCELER-
ATE EVERYTHING. THE SHOTS,
THE HITS, THE TEMPERS. BUT
THEY DON'T PUT THE PLAYERS ON
AN EQUAL FOOTING. QUITE THE
OPPOSITE. THEY EXAGGERATE
THEIR TALENTS AND TENDENCIES.
A LEVIATHAN DEFENSEMAN IS
GIVEN THE SPEED TO HUNT. THE
ELUSIVE FORWARD, THE SPEED
AND MANEUVERS TO SCORE AND
ESCAPE.

WHY THE INTENSITY?

life is a

WHY SUCH AN AGGRESSIVE SPORT? IT'S NOT THE PUCK, NOT
THE PRESSURE OF THREE ON ONES OR POWER PLAYS. THE
ANSWER LIES IN THOSE BLADES. SPEND SIXTY MINUTES A
NIGHT LIVING ON A RAZOR AND ASK THE QUESTION AGAIN...
GET HIT AT FULL SPEED BY THE GUY WHO HAS BEEN LINING
YOU UP FROM HIS BLUE LINE, AND SEE IF YOU'RE STILL
WONDERING WHY. REMEMBER THE TIME WE WATCHED THOSE
BLADES SLIT A GUY'S THROAT ON NATIONAL TV IF YOU EVER
FORGET HOW SHARP THAT EDGE IS.

contact sport

FLYING BY THE BALLS OF YOUR FEET

A climber hangs on a rock. He's up high, and an hour ago he felt good, strong. But his fingertips are now tortured, his tendons are cramped, and dreams of the summit have turned to questions of How? and If? There is nothing to be gained by waiting. **No short-cut.** It's a long way up, a longer way down, and a very high price to pay either way.

There is no time-out,

and
no bench to
retreat to.

It's simple.
You lose, you go home.

You can die doing this.
Forget humiliation. Both pride and
wounds heal. This is every seventh
game, every fourth and goal, every
double or nothing wrapped up in one
FINAL PLAY.

Life's not too short. It's just that you're dead for so long.

The meek shall inherit the earth.

They just better
stay the hell off the track.

All the excitement
of a trip to hell.

The race is won on the grid. Before the green. Before the checkered flag. It is won in the mind of the man who most clearly sees himself standing on the podium, spraying the crowd with champagne. The race is won as a child, before the contracts and paychecks. It is won in soapboxes at the end of the street.

Victory is rarely more than visualization. Simply, we get what we want, fight and pray for. Children dream only of great conquests, never of second place. It becomes their reality out of ignorance and innocence. They have not yet learned about limitations, and so they want it all. And a champion remembers the child's vision.

Don't have a hero. Loo[k]
Because if someone i[s]
the best you'll ever b[e]

After the eighth, the eye is cut. Not to heal it but for the man to see, to finish the fight.

The warrior doesn't fight out of aggression, hate or fear. He fights from a sense of responsibility and code. He lives in a world where wounds are medals and the weapons that inflict them are sacred. But these instruments are designed to do more than punish and defend. They have been crafted over generations to physically and spiritually guard his tribe, his country, and to settle age-old disputes of land, race and religion.

p to no one.
eading the way,
s second.

The warrior is not a soldier. While his fight is no more noble, it is much more symbolic. If a man falls to the canvas, his cause collapses for the moment. And if the man gets up, he lifts the weight of his world to its feet. If he is counted out, the only consolation for his corner is the promise of a rematch and the time to sharpen his weapons and abilities to a flawless point.

ONLY THOSE
WHO DARE TO LOSE,

WIN.

Beaten paths are for beaten men.

We take these risks, not to escape life,

He is temporary to everyone but himself. To his fans, he is an ideal. To team owners and managers, a commodity. To his competitors, an obstacle. **The tentative existence of an athlete is as ancient as man being thrown to the lions for the entertainment of kings.**

...but to prevent life from escaping us.

He is disposable, and to survive knowing this,

he must remain self-absorbed and motivated for

his own reasons. The desire to win must be his

passion alone, because he alone will live with the

outcome. That is the only permanent thing.

The best look at one's soul
is from beyond the edge, looking back.

When your life finally flashes before your eyes, you get one last look at all you've ever done...

and one last chance to regret everything you never tried.

The machine creates a unique dynamic in sport. It provides a third dimension—a less than entirely reliable partner that will turn the speed against itself and its pilot with little provocation. This manages to split the athlete's attention between two possible opponents.

Of the two, the machine may be the most formidable. It is just metal, oil and plastic, but it is relentless and has no capacity for compassion or mercy. Yet the machine seems aware and as interested in victory as its passenger. It will work toward it, with or without him. It is uncaring and only knows fatigue as an empty tank.

Think of

yourself as
invincible.
Believe
everything
is yours
for a price.
Some will
call it
foolish and
blame it
on the
innocence of
youth…
others
will just
call it
courage.

It wouldn't be
one man's dream if it wasn't
another man's possession.

You can't win the Game

when you're sitting on the bench.

He hit this ball ou[t] [of the]

park years before th[is] [on]

the swing. This ball f[lew over]

the fence a[t] [a game]

on a tattered Little League [field]

in the MIDDLE [OF] NOWHERE. The bases were

loaded then a[s] well, b[ut] they were

schoolbook[s] [a]nd lunch bags, [a]nd the bat

was crude[.] [O]ut of the park and

into the [c]rowd...into a neighbor's yard.

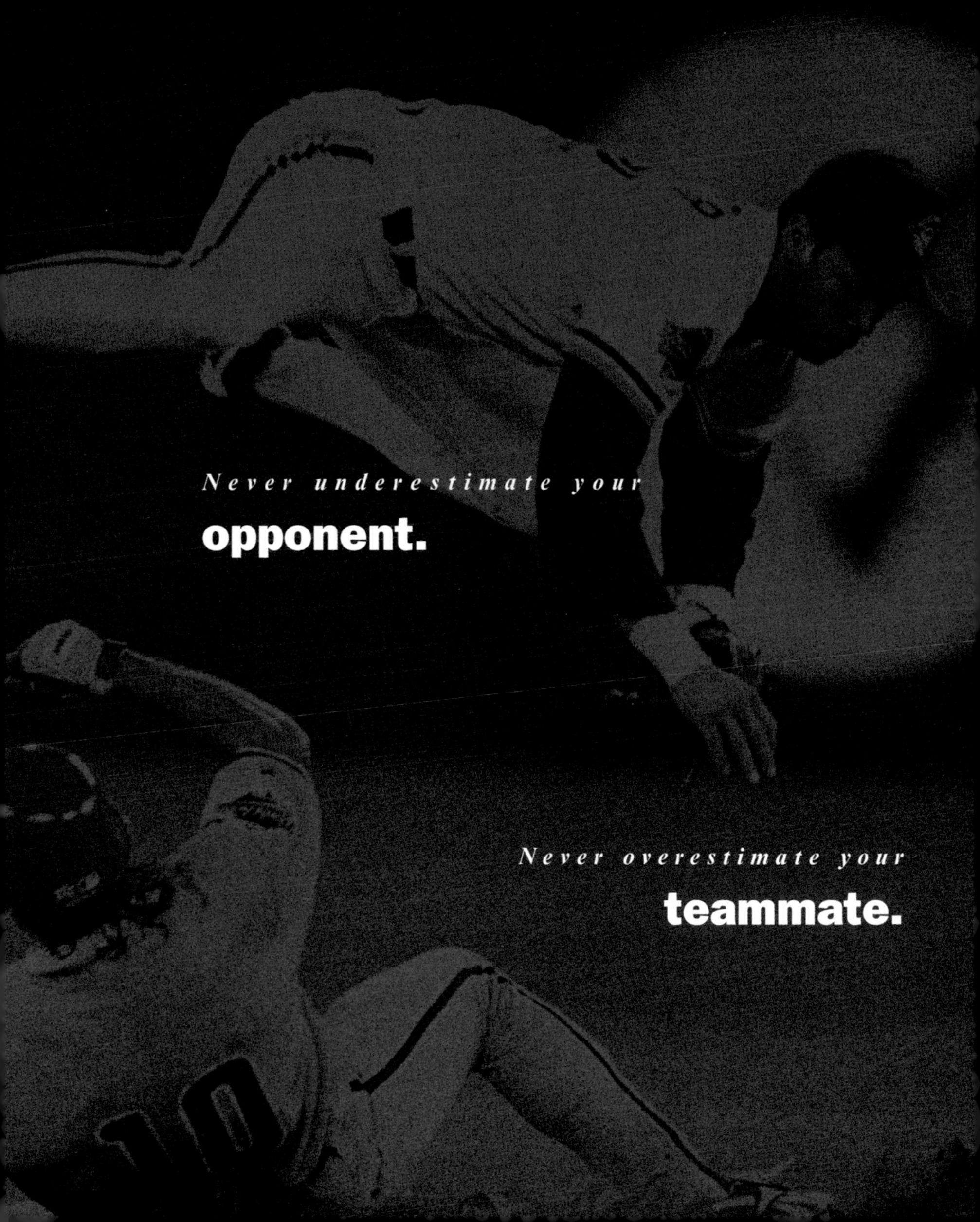

Never underestimate your

opponent.

Never overestimate your

teammate.

The Super Bowl.

It is civil war once a year, reenacted. It is North and South, and we choose sides to satisfy that which is only our nature. We love the fight. We need conflict to remain calibrated, and the big Game distills a year's worth into two halves, four quarters. It has become a fixture of American culture but it quenches a universal thirst. We need a foe, either real or imagined, against whom to test our worth. We need a prize… as simple as a ball or points on the board. So once a year we reduce our country to one hundred yards. We all take to the field, making the calls, blitzing, leading the drive. And, win or lose, we get our fix.

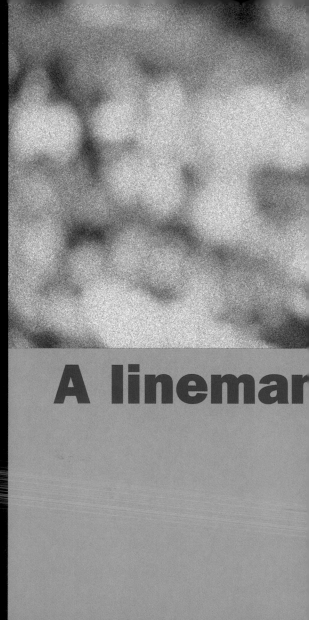

A lineman

hears the calls,

knows exactly the moment the ball is snapped from its place on the ground.

He won't see it, won't touch it. The play is not about him. It is never about

him. His world is the line between us and them, between invading and being

invaded. It begins with the man in motion and ends in collision with a man

of equal and opposite mass. Nothing more.

You'll never know what's on the other side

until you land there.

Second place is the first loser.

A competitor wants to win, to beat you. But an opponent doesn't care about the Game. He doesn't understand the rules and refs. He can't hear the whistle at the end of the play. He's not there for the point, the trophy or the crowd. And he certainly isn't looking for any sportsmanship awards at the end of the season. He wants just one thing. He wants to hurt you.

Dan Osman
Photograph by
Kevin Worrall

Michael Ho
Surfing Legend
Photograph by
Tim Mantoani

Ty Murray
Six-time world
all-around champion
cowboy
Photograph by
Mark Reis / PRCA

Michael Ho
Surfing Legend
Photograph by
Tim Mantoani

Ty Murray
Six-time world
all-around champion
cowboy
Photograph by
Tim Mantoani

Mike King
1993 world downhill
mountain bike
champion
Photograph by
Tim Mantoani

Glen Plake
Extreme skier
Photograph by
Larry Prosser

Trevor Linden
NHL All Star
Photograph by
Rick Stewart / Allsport

Stu Grimson
Detroit Red Wings
Photograph by
Al Bellow / Allsport

Marty Nothstein
1994 world champion,
track cycling
Photograph by
Tim Mantoani

Mike Siepel
Two-time world
champion, barefoot
waterskiing
Photograph by
Tim Mantoani

Photograph by
Tim Mantoani

Photograph by
John Mireles

John Force
NHRA funny car
champion
Photograph by
Paul Webb

Photograph by
John Mireles

Rick Mears
Four-time Indy 500
winner
Photograph by
Dan Boyd

Paul Tracy
Indy car driver,
Team Newman/Haas
Photograph by
Tony Di Zinno

Mike King
1993 world downhill
mountain bike
champion
Photograph by
Tim Mantoani

Photograph by
Tim Mantoani

Ivan Stewart
Baja 1000 legend,
Team Toyota
Photograph by
Marshall Williams

Photograph by
Tim Mantoani

Photograph by
Kevin Worrall

Jim Knaub
Wheelchair racer,
Five-time Boston
marathon winner
Photograph by
Tim Mantoani

Mike Kiedrowski
Motocross,
Team Kawasaki
Photograph by
Tim Mantoani

Mike Kiedrowski
Motocross,
Team Kawasaki
Photograph by
Tim Mantoani

Photograph by
Mike Powell / Allsport

Randy Ready
Philadelphia Phillies
Photograph by
Tim Mantoani

Jerome Bettis
St. Louis Rams
Photograph by
Tom Cooke

Photograph by
Jim Commentucci / Allsport

Sammy Duvall
World record holder,
waterski jumping
Photograph by
Tim Mantoani

Roberto Alomar
Toronto Blue Jays
Photograph by
Rick Stewart / Allsport

Photograph by
Tim Mantoani